AF375229

50
48
4
23
7
0
40
1
2
3
4
9
7
8
13
5
6
33
30
28

$$16 + 13 =$$

$$29 + 63 =$$

$$58 + 4 =$$

$$3 + 28 =$$

$$38 + 41 =$$

$$13 + 72 =$$

$$16 + 81 =$$

$$16 + 80 =$$

$$13 + 1$$

$$22 + 54 =$$

$$22 + 48 =$$

$$18 + 1$$

$22 = \bigcirc$

$23 + 6 = \bigcirc$

$2 + 2 = \bigcirc$

$16 + 36 = \bigcirc$

$2 + 8 = \bigcirc$

$1 + 44 = \bigcirc$

$1 + 89 = \bigcirc$

$4 + 5 = \bigcirc$

$1 + 23 = \bigcirc$

$26 + 3 = \bigcirc$

$18 + 45 = \bigcirc$

$13 + 20 = \bigcirc$

33 × 346
16 + 1234

GUS the PLUS
A Math Hero's Mission
843+26
23+364
By Jennifer Jones

In one classroom where chaos reigned,
The kids looked puzzled and bored.
Math problems stacked as high as the sky,
Till Gus the Plus leapt aboard.

4+3=
5+13=
+20=

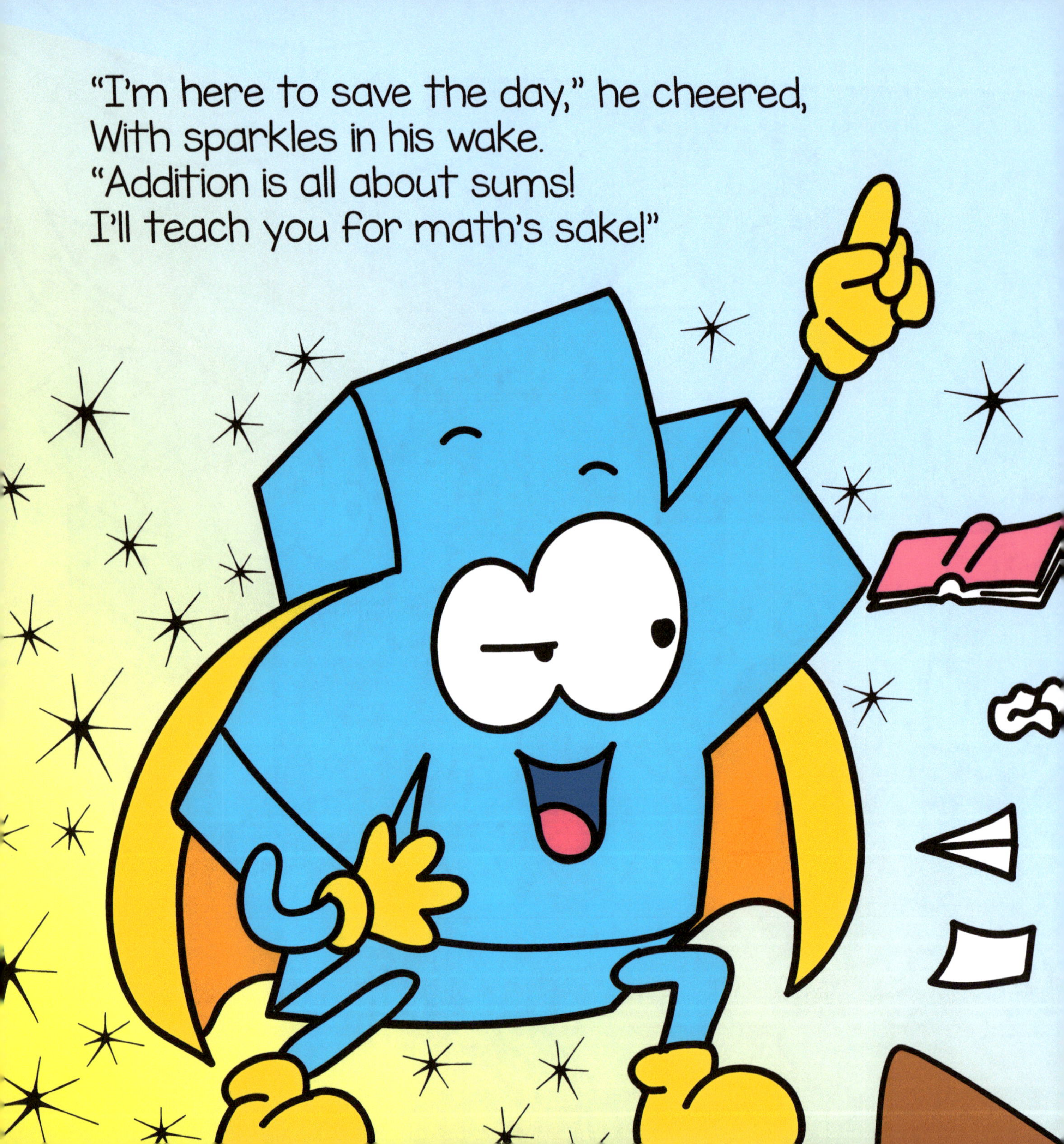

"I'm here to save the day," he cheered,
With sparkles in his wake.
"Addition is all about sums!
I'll teach you for math's sake!"

He grabbed some marbles from his bag,
"One plus one is our start!
Now tell me, quick, what is the sum?
Let's see who's math-smart!"

The kids all squinted with confused faces,
Till one proclaimed, "It's two!"
"Correct!" Gus shouted, "That's the sum!
And there's much more to do!"

"Here's a jar with two toy cars
That I bought from the store."
"Now add two more cars to the lot.
What's the total on the floor?"

"Four cars!" one shouted loudly,
And Gus gave them a wink.
"Addition's fun when we work together,
It's faster than you think!"

Next up, a plate of tasty snacks,
"There's three cookies for me and you.
Now I'll add three more brownies.
Adding this up is all that's left to do."

A kid stood tall with a clear answer,
"It's six!" he shouted out loud.
"You've got it right!" Gus clapped his hands,
"Great! I'm so proud!"

"Let's try with some clothes like hats,
And we'll add some scarves just for fun!
Three hats, plus two scarves –
How many do we have when we're done?"

HA HA
HA
HA
HA

A kid replied with a hearty laugh,
"Five is what we've got!
Yes, the total's five, all added up—
That's more than just a lot!"

Gus grabbed a bunch of jelly beans,
"Let's count ten, then add ten more.
Now tell me, kids, how many in all
Are waiting to be eaten in this jar?"

"Twenty!" shouted the class happily.
Gus gave a cheer of delight.
"You've worked hard today,
And you're absolutely right!"

Then Gus paused with a thoughtful grin,
"Addition solves it all!
From snacks to toys, it helps us win,
No problem is too small!"

So when you're counting stars at night,
Or snacks piled high to share,
Remember Gus and all he taught:
Math magic's everywhere.

+
18
+
+
5
16

Gus's Math Mission:

1. Gus has 3 marbles. He adds 4 more. How many marbles does Gus have now? _______________

2. There are 5 kids on swings and 6 more arrive. How many kids are swinging in total? _______________

3. Gus eats 2 cookies and adds 3 cupcakes to his plate. How many treats does he have to eat?

   ____

16 + 13 = ○

29 + 63 = ○

58 + 4 =

3 + 28 = ○

38 + 41 = ○

16 + 1

13 + 72 = ○

16 + 81 = ○

16 + 80 = ○

13 +

22 + 54 = ○

22 + 48 = ○

18 + 1

+22 = ◯

23+6 = ◯

2+2 = ◯

16+36 = ◯

2+8 = ◯

1+44 = ◯

1+89 = ◯

4+5 = ◯

11+23 = ◯

26+3 =

18+45 = ◯

13+20 = ◯